QUESTIONING HISTORY

The African American Slave Trade

Christine Hatt

WAYLAND

© 2003 White-Thomson Publishing Ltd

Produced for Hodder Wayland by
White-Thomson Publishing Ltd
2/3 St Andrew's Place
Lewes BN7 1UP

Other titles in this series:
The Causes of World War II
The Cold War
The Holocaust
The Western Front
Editor: Anna Lee
Designer: Derek Lee
Consultant: Howard Temperley
Proofreader: Philippa Smith
Picture research: Shelley Noronha, Glass Onion Pictures

Published in Great Britain in 2003 by Hodder
Wayland, an imprint of Hodder Children's Books.

This paperback edition published by Wayland in 2007,
an imprint of Hachette Children's Books.

The right of Christine Hatt to be identified as
the author has been asserted by her in accordance
with the Copyright, Designs and Patents Act 1988.

British Cataloguing in Publication Data
Hatt, Christine
   African-American Slave Trade. - (Questioning
History) 1. Slave trade - Africa - Juvenile
literature 2. Slave trade - America - Juvenile
literature
I. Title II. Lee, Anna
382.4'4'09

ISBN-10: 0 7502 5114 X
ISBN-13: 978 0 7502 5114 3

Printed in China

Hachette Children's Books
338 Euston Road, London NW1 3BH

Picture acknowledgements:
AKG *title page* 4, 5, 7, 10, 20, 29, 32, 54, 56;
Bridgeman 9, 30, 39; Topham 12, 13, 15, 22, 25,
28, 34, 40, 43; Mary Evans Picture Library 26, 27,
30; Corbis 36, 37, 45, 53; Hulton Archive *cover*
41, 50; Popperphoto 48, 57, 59.

Cover picture: A group of escaped slaves ouside a
cabin. Escaped slaves were known as contrabands
after the Union General Benjamin Butler
(1818-1893) announced that any slaves in land
controlled by the Union Army would be regarded
as contraband property.

CONTENTS

CHAPTER 1

Causes of Slavery

Beginning in the mid-fifteenth century and lasting over 400 years, the African-American slave trade became the largest forced migration in the history of the world. Experts estimate that during this long period, Europeans shipped about 12 million Africans across the Atlantic Ocean to the Americas against their will. This huge movement of people had immensely far-reaching consequences, both in the lands to which the slaves travelled and in the suffering continent that they left behind.

Enslaved Africans were transported to destinations in North America, South America and the islands of the Caribbean (see map page 16). A million or more died during the harsh sea crossing, while the survivors faced futures of great hardship. The details of slaves' lives varied over time and according to location. Most toiled in fields to bring in harvests of sugar cane, tobacco, cotton, rice and more. Others worked in the mansions of their wealthy masters as domestic slaves. Yet others developed specialist skills, for example as blacksmiths or cooks. But

BELOW *Buying slaves on the West African coast.*

LEFT *Slaves picking cotton in Georgia, a state of the American South. During the nineteenth century, cotton became such an important crop in the South that the region was known as the Cotton Kingdom.*

whatever their individual circumstances, slaves were all alike in one respect – they were not free, but the 'property' of their white owners.

The African-American slave trade reached its height in the late eighteenth century. In the 1780s, the trade's busiest decade, about 80,000 slaves were taken from Africa each year. But by that time, this grim commerce in human lives was under attack. Many white Christians had begun to regard the trade as an offence against God, and started to campaign for abolition. Slaves and former slaves had also organized abolitionist groups. Moral outrage was not the only force for change. By the late nineteenth century, profound economic and political developments in Europe and the Americas had also played their part in bringing the African-American slave trade, and slavery itself, to an end.

The vast scope of the slave trade, across time and continents, means there are many questions for historians to debate. Their discussions are not simply dry, academic arguments about the past. People of African descent now living in Europe and the Americas still feel the effects of their history. Likewise, Africa still bears the scars of European intervention. As a result, questions about the African-American slave trade are as relevant today as they have ever been.

WEST AFRICA IN THE PRE-EUROPEAN ERA

Most slaves transported to the Americas came from West and West Central Africa. These vast regions were divided into savannah and rainforest areas, and were inhabited by many different peoples. During the centuries before European arrival, both the lands and their inhabitants underwent major changes.

There had been trade links between North and West Africa since ancient times, and in about 300 CE the northern Berber people had begun to operate camel caravans across the Sahara Desert between the two regions. The Berbers took salt, horses, cattle and copper south, and kola nuts, ivory and gold north. To be successful traders, West Africans had to be well-organized. So, from about 600 CE, centrally controlled states grew up where North African desert met West African savannah.

Another force for change was Islam. Founded in Arabia during the seventh century, the faith spread rapidly west, establishing itself in North Africa by 750. Over the following centuries, Muslim merchants carried Islam south across the Saharan sands, and it was adopted by many of the new states.

? PEOPLE IN QUESTION

Askia Muhammad (c.1443–1538)

Askia Muhammad, also known as Askia the Great, led the Songhai empire from 1493 to 1528. In many ways he was a skilful ruler. He built an army and extended his lands east and north. He also restructured the government, improved the imperial finances and strengthened Islam, especially in cities. But some historians question Askia's greatness. They point out that his efforts to build a vast Islamic empire, and to enforce Islam among country people who followed traditional African religions, led to turmoil. Askia was deposed in 1528. When Morocco invaded in 1591, the Songhai empire was so divided that it collapsed. No empire emerged to replace it, leading some experts to claim that West Africa's entire future was damaged by Askia Muhammad and his successors.

STATES, EMPIRES AND KINGDOMS

Among the greatest of West Africa's early Islamic states were the Mali, Songhai and Kanem-Bornu empires. In more southerly areas, non-Islamic states developed, such as the rainforest kingdoms of Benin and Kongo. But although many West Africans were members of empires and kingdoms by the time Europeans arrived, thousands still belonged to societies without central rulers.

SLAVERY IN AFRICA

Slavery existed in West Africa long before the African-American slave trade developed. Prisoners of war and criminals were often enslaved by fellow Africans, then sold far from their homes. But unlike slaves in the Americas, they were usually able to improve their position through hard work. In some cases they could even shed their slave status. Slaves were also taken across the Sahara by Muslim traders: they were then sold in North Africa or exported to Europe and Asia. In East Africa, too, there was an Arab-run slave commerce.

RIGHT *This magnificent brass sculpture of a goddess's head was made in Benin during the sixteenth century CE.*

7

THE AMERICAS IN THE PRE-EUROPEAN ERA

Europeans did not establish permanent settlements in the Americas until the sixteenth century (see page 10). By then, over 300 American Indian peoples, such as the Mohawk and Cherokee, inhabited the lands north of Mexico, while two peoples, Arawaks and Caribs, lived on the islands of the Caribbean Sea. During the same era, the Aztecs dominated Central America, and the Incas ruled South America.

North America

Between 5 and 7 million people lived in North America during the immediate pre-European era, but lifestyles and languages varied widely across the continent. To study North American Indian peoples, experts divide them into ten cultural areas, in each of which men and women shared similar ways of life. So, for example, south-western peoples practised farming, while many Plains peoples lived by buffalo-hunting and plant-gathering. The north-eastern peoples, who were the first to come into contact with English settlers, lived by a mixture of farming, hunting and gathering that varied according to their exact location.

? EVENT IN QUESTION

The collapse of Cahokia

The Mississippian culture emerged in the south-east of North America during the late seventh century. Mississippians were particularly famous for building cities around flat-topped earth mounds that had temples on the top. The largest of these cities was Cahokia, which lay near present-day St Louis, Illinois. At its height, Cahokia contained more than 100 mounds and over 10,000 people. But by the sixteenth century, when the Spanish arrived, the city was deserted. The question for historians is whether Cahokia collapsed because farming could not support all its people, because disease caused mass deaths, or for some other reason.

The Caribbean Islands

In the fifteenth century, most Caribs occupied the southerly Caribbean islands known as the Lesser Antilles, which include Barbados and Grenada. They were a warlike people, who fought their Arawak neighbours. Most Arawaks lived in the Greater Antilles, that is northerly Caribbean islands such as Jamaica and

Cuba. They were usually less aggressive, had developed a hierarchical society led by chieftains, and worshipped their gods in
complex rituals.

Central and South America

The Aztecs arrived in Central America's Valley of Mexico during
the fourteenth century and settled in Tenochtitlán, which became
their capital. By the time of European conquest in the early sixteenth century, they had used their armies to build an empire of
over 10 million people. The Inca Empire of the Andes also grew
rapidly during the fifteenth century, until it stretched 4,000 km
down South America's west coast. But civil war had already
weakened this civilization by the time of European arrival.

Many South Americans did not, however, belong to empires
at all. Instead they lived in small, locally led groups that shared
much of their culture with neighbouring peoples. In rainforest
regions around the River Amazon, for example, many peoples
survived by catching fish and manatees, and by growing crops
such as manioc.

BELOW *Carib Indians on
the South American
mainland use bows and
arrows to catch fish and
other river creatures,
while colourful parrots
fly overhead.*

EUROPEAN SETTLEMENT

Vikings lived briefly in the Americas from about 1000 CE. But Europeans did not arrive to stay until the late fifteenth century. To them, this so-called New World offered the hope of great riches, land and power.

BELOW *Columbus's first landing place in the Americas was the island of San Salvador in the Bahamas, which he reached on 12 October 1492. This sixteenth-century engraving shows his arrival on another Caribbean island, Hispaniola, later the same year.*

First Contact

Spain was the first European country seriously to explore the Americas. By the late fifteenth century, newly united under Roman Catholic monarchs Ferdinand and Isabella, it had the money and the shipping technology to cross the Atlantic Ocean. It was Italian explorer Christopher Columbus who spurred the king and queen into action. Promising them the chance to spread their faith and to gain immense wealth, he persuaded them to pay for a westward voyage.

When Columbus set out in 1492, his aim was to reach Asia – Europeans did not then know that the Americas existed. But on 12 October, he landed in the Bahamas. During this and three later voyages, Columbus visited other islands, as well as Central and South America. At first, the Spanish who followed him just looked for gold on islands such as Cuba. But then some crossed to the mainland. In 1521, Hernán Cortés overthrew the Aztecs and in 1533, Francisco Pizarro defeated the Incas. Further east, the Portuguese reached Brazil in 1500.

North America

The Spanish went north, too, settling lands from California to Florida. From the sixteenth century, English people also claimed parts of North America. Some, such as the settlers of Virginia (1607), hoped to make their fortunes. But others emigrated to escape religious problems. The founders of Plymouth colony (1620), for example, had rejected Anglican beliefs. By 1733, there were thirteen English colonies on North America's east coast.

The French also settled parts of North America. They claimed regions in modern-day Canada during the sixteenth century and the Mississippi River valley during the seventeenth century.

? EVENT IN QUESTION

The treatment of Indians

Spanish settlers in the Americas treated the local populations with great brutality. The Indians also suffered outbreaks of European diseases such as measles to which they had no immunity. As a result millions died. All historians now accept that the terrible treatment of the Indians was wrong. But at the time, the question was hotly debated. Spanish priest Bartolomé de las Casas campaigned for Indian rights, and in his book *History of the Indies* (1552) denounced the abuses they endured:

Endless testimonies ... prove the mild ... temperament of the natives ... But our work was to exasperate, ravage, kill, mangle and destroy ...

However, in a formal discussion held before judges in Spain in 1548, Juan Ginés de Sepúlveda hit back. He claimed that Indians required:

... to be placed under the authority of civilized and virtuous princes and nations, so that they might learn from the might, wisdom and law of their conquerors to practise better morals ...

THE SPREAD OF SUGAR

Portuguese sailors had reached Africa some fifty years before they arrived in Brazil. It was on that great continent's west coast that they captured the first black slaves. And the reason? Sugar.

Europeans first grew sugar cane on Mediterranean islands such as Cyprus. When the Portuguese colonized São Tomé and other islands off Africa's west coast in the 1400s, they established sugar plantations there, too. At first, slaves from the Balkans and the trans-Saharan trade (see page 6) were used to cultivate the canes. But as European desire for sugar grew, labour supply could not meet demand. This demand increased in the 1500s, when the Portuguese began to grow sugar in Brazil, and the Spanish on Hispaniola.

BELOW The large structure on the left of this picture is the old slaving fort of Elmina. The fort still stands in modern-day Ghana and many people visit every year to see the terrible conditions in which slaves were held.

SLAVES FROM AFRICA

The Portuguese now decided to take slaves directly from West Africa. In 1441, a sailor kidnapped the first ten, and other men soon followed his example. Forty years later, the Portuguese built Elmina, a fort on the west African coast, to protect their gold and slaves from both other Europeans and Africans. Slowly, a trading pattern developed. In general, Europeans did not go far inland to find slaves. Instead they bought them from African merchants, who purchased or seized them some distance from the coast, then marched them to the sea.

A CHANGING SITUATION

By the early 1600s, about 350,000 slaves had left Africa and the Portuguese were exporting some 25,000 tonnes of sugar to Europe each year. Meanwhile, the Spanish were sending home vast quantities of silver and gold from South American mines. But until this time, people from other European lands had played little official part in the slave trade.

In the seventeenth century, this situation altered as England, France, Holland and Denmark gained American colonies. England, for example, had nine colonies in North America by the mid-1600s, and had seized Barbados and other Caribbean islands. Soon, European-controlled sugar production spread through the West Indies and demand for slaves soared.

BELOW *After retiring from his trading exploits at sea, John Hawkins became treasurer of the English navy.*

? PEOPLE IN QUESTION

John Hawkins (1532-1595)

Many English sailors attacked Spanish ships carrying treasure from the Americas. Among them was John Hawkins. However, he did not deal only in gold and silver. Instead, in 1562, he sailed to West Africa and became the first Englishman to capture black slaves. Later he sold all 300 to Spanish planters on Hispaniola.

Hawkins made two more slaving voyages and some historians claim that he played an important part in establishing the English slave trade. Others question this view, saying he was just a money-seeking adventurer, as his own declaration, made to Queen Elizabeth I, suggests:

My sovereign good lady and mistress, the voyage I pretend [plan] is to lade [take on board] negroes in Guinea [part of West Africa] and sell them in the West Indies in truck of [exchange for] gold, pearls and emeralds.

NORTH AMERICAN SLAVERY

The growth of the slave trade during the seventeenth and eighteenth centuries was prompted largely by the 'Sugar Revolution' in the Caribbean. But North American developments also added to the relentless demand for slaves from Africa.

Indentured Labourers

Many early English settlers in North America employed indentured labourers to grow crops such as tobacco and rice in their fields. These workers were poor white people who, in return for a free transatlantic voyage from England, agreed to work in North America for nothing but their keep for several years. This system worked well until the 1680s, when demand began to outstrip supply. There were two main reasons. First, the English population of North America had grown rapidly, which meant that the need for indentured labourers also increased quickly. Second, the turmoil caused by the English Civil War earlier in the century had faded, so people were far less eager to make the journey westward.

A New Source

English settlers had already tried and failed to make American Indians work for them, and now the supply of workers from England was drying up. They urgently needed another source of labour.

Twenty Africans, the first to reach North America, had been brought to Virginia across the Atlantic by a Dutch sea captain in 1619. At the time, it was not worth the expense or the potential conflict with other slaving nations to import many more. But by the late seventeenth century, the situation was very different. English slave ships were now making frequent transatlantic journeys to Barbados and to Jamaica, which had been seized from Spain in 1655. The ships could easily make another stop on their journey to bring Africans to mainland America. So, with increasing regularity, they did.

EVENT IN QUESTION

Racism – cause or effect?

Many historians debate whether racism was a cause or an effect of slavery. People who argue it was a cause say Europeans had a low opinion of black people from the start. This was because they did not look like whites, did not share European cultural values and were not Christians.

Experts who argue racism was an effect of slavery point out that it developed only over time. At first, blacks in North America were often able to socialise with whites and had a reasonable chance of buying their freedom. But from the late 1600s, as the number of slaves and slave laws increased, prejudice became widespread. There is also a third view, expressed in this quotation from *American Slavery* (1993) by American historian Peter Kolchin:

... the most appropriate question is not whether slavery caused prejudice or prejudice caused slavery ... but rather how slavery and prejudice interacted to create the particular set of social relationships that existed in the English mainland colonies.

ABOVE *Frightened and far from home, African slaves climb from the rowing boats that have brought them to shore from the ships in the distance. Meanwhile, white men prepare to buy and sell this human cargo.*

EUROPE IN AFRICA

The rise in slave traffic during the 1600s and on into the following century profoundly altered the nature of slaving in Africa. It also brought thousands more Europeans to the continent's shores in search of adventure and profit.

During the seventeenth century, many European governments began to sponsor slave-trading expeditions, and set up companies to do this barbarous work. English king Charles II personally chartered the Royal African Company in 1663. All these companies built forts in West Africa, so that there were soon over fifty European 'castles' on or near the coast (see map). Among the most important were Elmina, which the Dutch took over in 1637, Christiansborg, completed by the Danes in 1661, and Cape Coast, occupied by the English from 1665.

BELOW *This map shows the major European forts on the coast of 18th-century West Africa. These 'castles' often passed from the control of one country to another as national fortunes changed.*

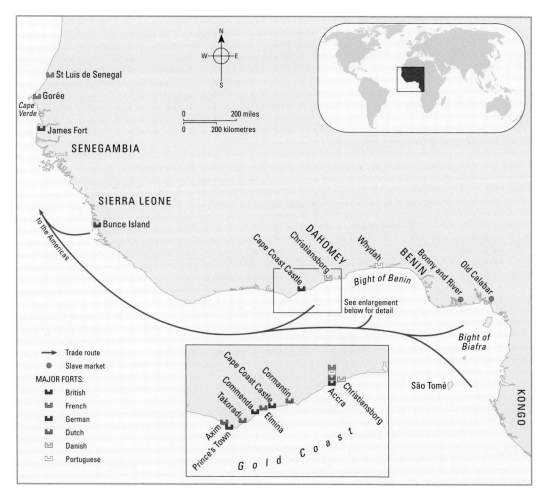

The new arrivals followed the Portuguese pattern of staying near their forts and using African or Afro-European middlemen to supply them with bought or kidnapped slaves. Nevertheless, many Europeans still caught diseases such as malaria and yellow fever. About a quarter of those who went to Africa in the early days of slaving died within a year of arrival. That is why Africa became known as the white man's grave.

SUPPLY AND DEMAND

Although Europeans were often far from the places where people were first enslaved, they were responsible for what happened. It was their constant demand for slaves, and the supply of guns, alcohol and other goods they provided in exchange, that raised slaving to a new pitch. But while most Africans lived in fear, a few exploited the situation for material gain. For example some chiefs started wars, fought with European guns, so that they could sell prisoners into slavery. They also invented new 'crimes' so that they could exchange the guilty for European wares.

? EVENT IN QUESTION

African involvement

There is an ongoing debate about the extent of African involvement in the slave trade. The question is complex, but careful study has shown there is no simple answer. Rather, involvement varied from region to region. The kings of Benin, for example, severely restricted slave exports. But the kings of Dahomey, to the west, traded enthusiastically with slavers, sent their army on slave raids and grew rich from the profits.

Documents from the era highlight the variety of responses. In 1526 Mbemba Nzinga, a ruler of the Kongo, wrote to the King of Portugal to protest against slaving. He explained that merchants were:

... taking every day our natives, sons of the land and sons of our noblemen ... and our relatives [so that] *our country is becoming completely depopulated, and Your Highness should not agree with this nor accept it as in your service.*

Other rulers were less scrupulous, as one African traveller explained:

The Kings are so absolute, that upon any slight pretense of offense committed by their subjects, they order them to be sold for slaves without regard to rank or profession.

17

ACROSS THE ATLANTIC

Enslavement was only the beginning of a terrifying ordeal for millions of West Africans. Once captured or purchased, they faced a lengthy journey to the coast, and a grim voyage across the Atlantic Ocean.

Slavers led their captives to the coast in groups of about 150. Chained to prevent escape, the slaves often had to walk for hundreds of kilometres and sometimes also to travel by boat along mighty rivers such as the Niger. About 40 per cent died en route. At journey's end, the slaves were sold to European traders. The Europeans wanted only strong, healthy men and women, so inspected captives closely before buying.

Before their transatlantic voyages began, many slaves were kept in the dark, airless dungeons of European forts. However, as slaving became big business, other arrangements also developed. The official slaving companies were originally monopolies. But as demand soared, governments let private companies transport slaves, too. Having no forts, these companies held slaves on ships until they were ready to sail.

? EVENT IN QUESTION

The African aftermath

The effects of the slave trade on Africa were immense, in terms of both personal suffering and lasting damage to the continent as a whole. No serious historian disputes that the trade was terrible. But there are differences of opinion about the extent to which it was responsible for the aftermath in Africa. In the book *African History* (1995), American historian Philip Curtin sums up his view as follows:

The sheer physical destructiveness of the trade was not significant enough to produce a general and striking difference in social health and progress between areas where the slave trade was prevalent and those where people suffered only from the usual run of war, plague, and famine.

In the book *Transatlantic Slavery* (1994), however, British historian Stephen Small makes a far harsher judgement:

... the countries of the West have relentlessly exploited Africa and African people. Millions of Africans were murdered, millions more violently kidnapped and enslaved ... and African societies totally ransacked ... slavery and colonialism created the circumstances which confine Africans and African nations to the worst conditions experienced by any people in the world today.

Ocean Crossing

The holds of slaving ships during sea crossings were a terrible sight. Their decks were rarely more than 1.5 metres high, but even these cramped quarters were often divided in two by horizontal platforms. As a result, slaves could not stand or sometimes even turn. To add to the discomfort, most slaves, especially males, were chained hand and foot.

There was worse. The facilities provided for going to the toilet were completely inadequate – often just a few buckets that most slaves could not in any case reach. As a result, the decks were soon awash with human waste, and diseases such as dysentery spread. In the early days of slaving, up to 40 per cent of slaves died on board ship during their transatlantic voyages, which lasted anything from six to sixteen weeks.

BELOW *The slave trade was often called the triangular trade, because of the three main sections, called passages, of slaving voyages. From the late seventeenth century, slaving became more of a rectangular trade with an additional stop in the West Indies.*

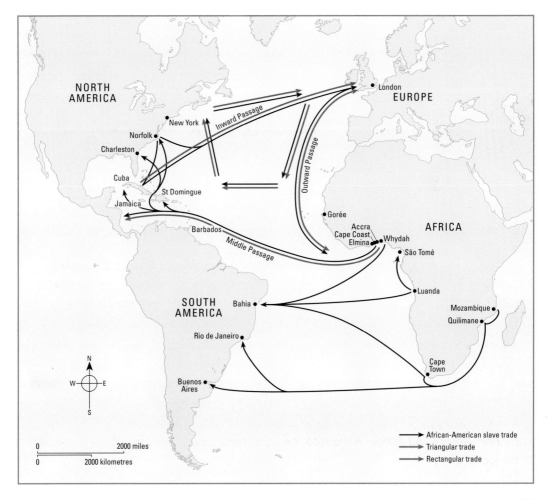

CHAPTER 2

The Slave Experience

Whether they landed on Caribbean islands or the American mainland, survivors of the Atlantic crossing faced more horrors in their new lives. On arrival, slaves were sold or handed to people who had pre-purchased them. Those for sale had again to endure physical examinations by potential owners. Slaves not bought quickly were sold at auctions on land. These were known as scrambles because planters simply grabbed the slaves they wanted.

SEASONING

The new slaves were disorientated and often deeply depressed. The slave-owners' concern was not, however, to make them happy, but to make them profitable. So they began the process of

BELOW *A nineteenth century slave sale in Richmond. This town is in Virginia, one of the North American colonies, where thousands of slaves worked in tobacco fields.*

'seasoning' or 'breaking in'. Above all, this meant introducing the slaves to the harsh labour demanded of them in the fields. However, it also involved efforts to detach the slaves from their African past, for example by making them adopt European names and speak European languages.

SLAVE SOURCES

As time passed, slaves came to the Americas from more and more areas of Africa. At first, most were from Senegambia, just south of the Sahara. But as demand increased, slavers pushed farther south and inland. In the eighteenth century, Angola and the Kongo produced more slaves than anywhere else – almost 38 per cent. Other major sources were the Bights of Benin and Biafra. But one factor was constant – more male than female slaves always came from Africa. In total, the ratio was about two to one, but in the early years it was far higher.

? **EVENT IN QUESTION**

Slave resistance

Most North American Indian peoples avoided enslavement. By contrast, African slavery lasted for 400 years. Some experts who questioned why Indian and African experiences were so different suggested that Africans had a 'slave mentality'. This is explained in *A People's History of the United States* by American Howard Zinn:

Some historians have painted a picture ... of a slave population made submissive by their condition; with their African heritage destroyed, they were ... made into ... "a society of helpless dependents."

Research shows this idea is false. Africans were at a great disadvantage over North American Indian peoples because they were not on home ground. They also faced terrible punishments for resistance. But they did resist. Some jumped overboard during the Atlantic crossing, others ran away or worked deliberately slowly. A few organized revolts. Historians Stephen Small and James Walvin sum up this idea in *Transatlantic Slavery* (1994):

Though many Africans were murdered, and many others psychologically smothered by [whites], the collective will of Africans refused to accept white domination. An understanding of resistance demonstrates the variety and vitality of the African spirit. European enslavement of Africans certainly victimized them; but it did not leave them with a victim mentality. Africans were not victims, but survivors.

SLAVES IN THE AMERICAN NORTH

Some 661,000 slaves were brought to North America from West Africa, just 5.5 per cent of the approximately 12 million total slaves taken forcibly across the Atlantic. The particular conditions on the mainland made their lives very different from those of slaves on the Caribbean islands (see page 26). The slave ways of life that grew up in the American North (the northern colonies of the mainland) were also substantially different from those that emerged in the American South (the southern colonies of the mainland).

BELOW The Pilgrims were English puritans who in 1620 crossed the Atlantic in the Mayflower. They had hoped to begin a new life in Virginia but due to a navigational error settled in New England instead.

New England

New England was the collective name given to the most north-easterly colonies (now states) of North America, including Massachusetts. By the early eighteenth century, slavery had been legalized throughout this region. However, it had few slaves

because most of the inhabitants were English Puritans, who liked to tend their own land. In 1750, for example, the slave population of Massachusetts was just 2.2 per cent of the total. Puritans did not necessarily have a moral objection to slaving, however. When the sale of slaves between states became widespread in the early nineteenth century (see page 45), many played a significant part in this trade.

The Middle Colonies

New York, New Jersey and Pennsylvania were known as the Middle Colonies of the American North, and had likewise all legalized slavery by the early 1700s. Here, ownership of slaves was more common, but few people possessed more than two. Of the three colonies, New York had by far the highest slave population – 14.3 per cent of the total in 1750. As this region had many towns, most slaves worked as house servants or specialist staff such as grooms, but some were agricultural labourers, for example, on New York wheat farms.

WHAT IF...

The American North had been more like the American South?

The fact that slave populations in the American North were far lower than in the agricultural South (see pages 24-25) had important effects. In the North, slaves normally lived in small groups. They also came into regular, close contact with whites, in their homes or their fields. As a result, they quickly adopted some aspects of white American culture.

In the South, by contrast, most slaves lived in far larger groups on big plantations. Many had relatively little contact with their white masters, and so kept their African character for much longer. In parts of Georgia and South Carolina, some spoke a language called Gullah, a mixture of African tongues that most whites could not understand.

Over time, the fact that the North was not dependent on slave labour like the South hardened the divisions between the two regions. These divisions led to the American Civil War (see pages 46-51), which in turn led to the abolition of slavery in the USA. So if the North had been more like the South, slavery might have continued across the country for far longer.

SLAVES IN THE AMERICAN SOUTH

The American South, from Delaware down to Georgia, was the heartland of slavery in North America, and slave ownership became a defining characteristic of the rich white planters who flourished in its colonies. The South had two distinct areas, the Upper South and the Deep South. Slavery was first established in the Upper South, especially Maryland and Virginia. These were tobacco-growing colonies, where slavery was legal from the early 1660s and landowners used many slaves to work their plantations. By 1750, slaves made up nearly 44 per cent of Virginia's population. Tobacco, once considered a weed by Europeans, became a major export, but from the mid-1700s, the crop often failed because the soil had been too intensively farmed. Partly as a result, sales slumped and many planters turned to grain crops and cattle farming instead.

Slave plantations became an important feature of life in the Deep South, especially North and South Carolina and Georgia, from the early 1700s. At first the principal crops were rice and indigo, a dye plant. Later, cotton also became a major product (see

? PEOPLE IN QUESTION

Southern slave-owners

There is a major debate among slavery experts about a whole class of people: Southern planters. Some historians, such as American Eugene D. Genovese, have argued that they were not capitalists, whose main aim was to make a profit. Rather they were like feudal lords, who enjoyed power over others. To them, slaves were not primarily money-making tools, but signs of status. This is how Genovese sums up this view:

The planters were ... quasi-aristocratic landowners [aristocrat-like landowners] *who had to adjust their economy and ways of thinking to a capitalist world market. Their society ... represented the antithesis* [opposite] *of capitalism.*

Other experts, particularly Americans Robert W. Fogel and Stanley L. Engerman, have argued Southern planters *were* capitalists. In *Time on the Cross* (1974), for example, they use statistics to suggest Southern planters, like Northern factory-owners, both tried and managed to make a profit:

The demonstration that an investment in slaves was highly profitable ... throws into doubt the contention [argument] *that slaveholders were* [an] *... uncommercial class which subordinated profit to considerations of power* [and] *life-style ...*

pages 44-45). The proportion of slaves was high – almost 61 per cent of South Carolina's population in 1750 – and ships regularly brought more from Africa to the coastal cities of Charleston, which became the state capital, and Savannah.

The Task System

In the 1700s, a method of working known as the task system developed in the Deep South, especially the rice-growing coastal regions of Georgia and South Carolina. Each morning, slaves were given a fixed task to complete under the eye of stern, usually black slave-drivers. But as soon as it was finished, they were free to leave the fields. This system encouraged slaves to work fast, while making it easy for masters to identify anyone who had done their task badly. It also allowed slaves to spend time relaxing, tending their own gardens, or selling their own crops at market.

BELOW *Slaves on this plantation, in the Deep South state of Mississippi, wade through ripe, waist-high cotton. Some of the most important cotton plantations in the state had poetic names such as Willow Dale, but depended on exploitative slave labour for their success.*

SLAVES IN THE CARIBBEAN

More Africans were taken to the Caribbean than to anywhere else in the Americas – some 40 per cent of the total. (About 38 per cent went to Portuguese-ruled Brazil.) The Caribbean system of slavery varied according to whether Britain, France or Spain was in control. In theory at least, France and Spain granted slaves more rights than in Britain. But throughout the region, most slaves worked on sugar plantations.

ABOVE *A nineteenth century sugar plantation in the West Indies. The owner's grand house can be seen top left, above the rows of simple slave cabins.*

A Harsh Life

Life on the plantations was harsh. Slaves were woken at about four in the morning. Within an hour, at most two, they had to be at work. Field slaves were divided into gangs according to age and strength. The most able men and women belonged to the First Gang. It did the heaviest work, such as hacking down sugar canes. The Second Gang cleared the fields of debris. The Third Gang, usually children and the old, did light tasks such as feeding animals.

The gang system also operated in the plantation factories, where the cane was crushed to extract its juice, then the juice boiled to obtain sugar crystals. Some of the sugar was also treated to produce sticky molasses and potent rum. The first six months of the year was the busy harvesting season. During that time, First Gang slaves often worked until sundown in the fields, then went straight on to the factories.

Caribbean Society

White planters on the Caribbean islands were hugely outnumbered by their black slaves. By 1713, the average ratio in the English colonies was four blacks to every white, but on some islands it was ten to one. Some planters built great houses, where they served fine food and wines to their guests. But many Europeans rarely visited their plantations, instead paying managers to deal with slaves and to endure the humid tropical climate.

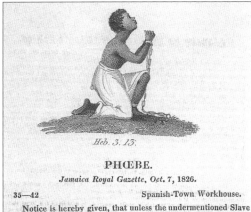

Heb. 3. 13.

PHŒBE.

Jamaica Royal Gazette, Oct. 7, 1826.

35—42   Spanish-Town Workhouse.

Notice is hereby given, that unless the undermentioned Slave is taken out of this Workhouse, prior to Monday the 30th day of October next, she will on that day, between the hours of 10 and 12 o'Clock in the forenoon, be put up to Public Sale, and sold to the highest and best bidder, at the Cross-Keys Tavern, in this Town, agreeably to the Workhouse Law now in force, for payment of her fees.

PHŒBE, a Creole, 5 feet 4½ inches, marked NELSON on breasts, and I O on right shoulder, first said to one Miss Roberts, a free Black, in Vere, secondly, to Thomas Oliver, Esq. St. John's, but it is very lately ascertained that her right name is Quasheba,

ABOVE *Slaves were often bought and sold like goods. This 1826 advertisement for a slave first appeared in a newspaper on the Caribbean island of Jamaica, but was later reproduced in an anti-slavery publication.*

? EVENT IN QUESTION

Birth and death

From the 1720s, the number of slaves in North America grew by natural increase, that is by slaves having children. But this did not happen in the Caribbean, where it was necessary to keep bringing large numbers of slaves from Africa to maintain the slave population. Experts are not sure why this difference developed. Was it caused by a high *birth* rate in North America or a high *death* rate in the Caribbean?

Caribbean death rates were high – about 5 per cent of the population per year in early nineteenth-century Jamaica, for example. Reasons included the intensity of work on sugar plantations, poor diet and the high number of African-born slaves, who often failed to survive long after arrival. Studies have, however, shown that death rates in North America were similar.

In contrast, the difference in birth rates was significant. By the 1800s, the rate among North American slaves was 80 per cent higher than among Jamaicans. One reason may be that the Caribbean remained culturally African for longer. Unlike American-born slaves, African women breast-fed for two or three years. As breast-feeding reduces fertility, this may have been partly responsible for the low birth rate.

SLAVE CODES

Slave-owners attempted to use the law to make slaves obey their every wish. In the same way, they tried to strip slaves of all their rights. Slave codes were groups of laws designed to regulate slaves' lives. The first British code developed in seventeenth-century Barbados. Codes were then introduced in Jamaica and the mainland colony of Virginia before spreading elsewhere. All slave codes were wide-ranging. In particular, they established slaves' status as property and banned them from learning to read or write and from owning property themselves. Some also banned slave marriages, but as time passed, these were allowed if owners gave their approval. The codes also forbade slaves to leave their plantations without permission and, through fear of rebellion, to meet in large groups.

Some code-makers tried to justify the cruel laws they introduced. South Carolina's code, for example, declared that it was because slaves had 'wild, savage natures' that they were 'wholly unqualified to be governed by the [usual] laws, customs and practices of this Province.'

BELOW *A chaplain from the Freedmen's Bureau (see page 53) marries a black soldier and his wife. This wedding took place in 1866 just after the nationwide abolition of slavery in the USA.*

Slave Punishments

Punishments for running away, taking part in organized rebellions, or breaking any other laws were generally severe. It was common for masters to strike slaves repeatedly with leather whips or, especially in North America, to beat them with paddles. These were pieces of leather-covered wood about 40 centimetres long that inflicted pain without leaving a mark. If a court judged a slave guilty of a serious crime such as burglary, sexual assault or murder – slave cases were rarely heard by juries – punishments were even harsher. They included mutilations, such as amputation of the fingers, and death.

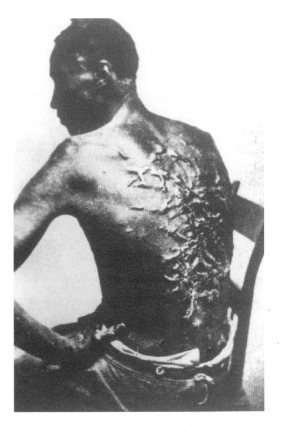

RIGHT *The scars of an escaped slave from Louisiana.*

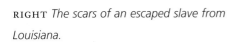

EVENT IN QUESTION

A change of heart?

From the late eighteenth century, planters in North America and the Caribbean began to punish their slaves less harshly than before. Slave-owners also began to think about their slaves in a different way. They were no longer savages to be kept under control, but childlike creatures who needed the guiding hand of a father figure.

Historians have long questioned why these changes happened. In North America, one reason was the growing number of Creoles, the name given to American-born slaves. They grew up knowing what was required of them, so planters did not need to impose such strict discipline on them as on Africans. In addition, during the American Revolution (see page 32) planters began to think about their rights as citizens of the newly created USA. This led some to think that slaves should have rights, too.

In British colonies, it was largely pressure from abolitionists that made some planters mend their ways. The 1807 abolition of the slave trade (not slavery) also led to government limits on punishments. But these limits were high – a slave might still receive up to 39 lashes. In the Caribbean, as in North America, slaves were kept in place by violence and the threat of violence for many years after abolition.

FAMILY, FAITH AND CULTURE

Slaves fought tirelessly against whites' onslaught on their rights. Three of the great 'weapons' they used were family, faith and culture.

Family Networks

Family networks were important in West Africa, so slaves valued family ties. At first, when male slaves far outnumbered females, it was hard for slaves to build families. This was of little concern to masters, especially in the Caribbean. If slaves did not pair off and

BELOW *Slave mothers were often forced to return to work while their children were still very young.*

? EVENT IN QUESTION

Family-building

The importance of slave families is a question much discussed by historians. Some experts argue that, by building their own strong communities, slaves were able to assert their independence and to enjoy a life their masters could not control. Other experts, however, point out that slaves did not have total control over their family lives. Masters often interfered in the upbringing of slave children, disrupted families by selling slaves and sexually exploited women. There is also a third argument that includes aspects of both these ideas, and that seeks, too, to encourage a realistic view of slaves' family lives. Peter Kolchin in his book *American Slavery* (1993) (see page 15), expresses this view as follows:

Slaves struggled against overwhelming odds to build decent lives for themselves and took pleasure when they could in their friends and families ... Slaves successfully resisted being turned into docile, obedient creatures of their masters' will; they did not turn the "slave community" into utopia [an ideal world].

produce children to replace themselves, it was a simple matter to bring more from Africa. Slowly, however, slaves did create new families. Particularly in North America, many made strong marriages that collapsed only when a slave-owner sold one partner. Many also had large families – women in the American South bore an average of seven children. Most children grew up with their mothers, and many with their fathers, too. But men were more likely to be sold or to live away from the family home on another plantation. Family networks did not include only close or blood relatives. Many aunts, uncles and cousins, real or honorary, also formed part of the relationship webs that supported parents and their children.

Faith and Culture

African slaves brought to the Americas a belief in God and in good and evil spirits. They also believed it was possible to communicate with these spirits, and in the Caribbean developed obeah, a religion with rituals designed to do so. In French-ruled Louisiana and St Domingue (modern day Haiti), voodoo emerged. It combined African beliefs with Roman Catholicism.

As time passed, Christianity spread among slaves. The growing number of American-born slaves were themselves more open to Christian ideas than those from Africa. But following two North American religious revivals known as Great Awakenings, during the mid-1700s and early 1800s, many planters also decided it was their moral duty to spread Christianity among their slaves. The push for change in the Caribbean came mainly from British missionaries.

By the 1830s, many slaves were Christians. But they emphasized different aspects of their faith from their masters. To them, Christianity did not so much demand obedience as offer hope, and they worshipped God fervently to show their gratitude for his promise of deliverance.

Although many adopted their enslavers' religion, slaves tried to ensure the survival of African culture. In the slave quarters, they shared music, dances and folk tales that joined them in spirit to their ancestors across the Atlantic.

CHAPTER 3

Changes in the Slave Trade

THE AMERICAN REVOLUTION

Until the mid-eighteenth century, most whites in North America accepted Britain's right to rule over them. But then came the American Revolution. From 1756 to 1763, Britain fought the Seven Years' War against the French in North America. It won, and gained many French territories. However, the fighting left Britain with massive debts. From 1764, the British parliament therefore introduced many new taxes for Americans to pay.

Americans were outraged at these financial demands, and also objected to the continuing presence of British troops on American soil. Matters came to a head on 16 December 1773, when people protesting against the British tax on tea invaded ships in Boston Harbour and threw 340 tea chests overboard.

BELOW *This eighteenth century painting portrays the 1775 Battle of Bunker Hill. Fought in Massachusetts, this was the first major clash between Americans and British during the American Revolution.*

In response, Britain passed the 1774 Coercive Acts, which allowed it to interfere even further in American affairs.

Many Americans now asked themselves why the British parliament, which they did not elect and in which they were not represented, should have such power over them? Eventually, on 19 April 1775, their anger led to war. Then, on 4 July 1776, the Americans issued the Declaration of Independence. It spelled out their wish to rule themselves as a republic. The American army was victorious and in 1783, the last British soldiers left the newly free country soon to be known as the United States of America (USA).

Slaves and the Revolution

By the 1770s, there were some 500,000 slaves in North America. About 5,000 fought in the American rebel army against the British. But far more fought alongside the British, some of whose leaders had offered them freedom in return. Thousands of other slaves took the chance to escape during the confusion that the fighting caused.

? PEOPLE IN QUESTION

Thomas Jefferson (1743-1826)

Thomas Jefferson, who became the USA's third president, was the main author of the Declaration of Independence. It contained the ringing statement that 'all men are created equal'. Yet Jefferson's treatment of black people has led experts to question whether he really believed these noble words.

In its final form, the Declaration did not mention the slave trade. But in his first draft, Jefferson called it an 'execrable commerce'. Other writings by Jefferson also suggest he wished to end slavery. In *Notes on the State of Virginia* (1785), for example, he stated:

The spirit of the slave [is] rising from the dust ... the way I hope preparing ... for a total emancipation.

But despite these views, Jefferson kept slaves all his life. Eventually, he also decided that emancipation would ruin the South's economy, so did not even free his own slaves. In 1805, he famously declared:

I have long since given up the expectation of any early provision for the extinction of slavery among us.

33

THE FIRST EMANCIPATION

BELOW *This painting by John Turnbull shows the signing of the Declaration of Independence in 1776.*

In the aftermath of the American Revolution, anti-slavery feeling steadily increased. In northern states especially, growing numbers of people asked themselves how a country that boasted of its devotion to liberty and equality could continue to accept this evil institution.

Anti-slavery Action

Feeling soon turned into action. Many people from the North formed anti-slavery groups such as New York's Manumission Society (1785). Some, especially Quakers, set their own slaves free. Slaves and free blacks (see page 36) played a significant part in promoting abolition. They made many speeches to state governments, as well as writing powerful letters and articles in support of their cause.

The campaigning paid off. In 1777, the northern state of Vermont had become the first to ban slavery, and was soon followed by others. In 1804, New Jersey became the last state in the North to prohibit slave-holding (see box). These northern slavery bans, collectively known as the First Emancipation, did not all come into effect immediately. Some states, such as Pennsylvania, introduced a process of gradual emancipation.

? EVENT IN QUESTION

Morality or Practicality –
Why did the North abolish slavery?

Many eighteenth-century Americans, and particularly the religious, opposed slavery because it was morally wrong. But experts have shown that the North did not abolish slavery purely because of moral concerns.

In fact, there were practical economic reasons for emancipating slaves in the North. Few people there had large plantations that needed hundreds of fieldworkers, so there was simply not the demand for slaves that existed in the South. What is more, poor white Northerners objected to slavery because they could not compete in the job market with people who received no wages for their labours. The importance of economic arguments is also shown by the fact that the northern states with most slaves – in other words, that were most likely to suffer damaging economic effects from emancipation – abolished slavery last. New York did not free its slaves until 1799 and New Jersey until 1804. Even then they passed laws that permitted only gradual emancipation.

Southern Resistance

In the southern states, the situation was more complex. Some planters, especially in the Upper South, shared northern unease at slavery and freed their own slaves. But private acts were not matched by public commitment – no southern state government declared slavery illegal.

The slave trade did, however, come to an end during this era. When the US constitution was drafted in 1787, Southerners had forced the inclusion of a clause saying that the trade would not be prohibited before 1808. A law banning the import of slaves from the beginning of that year was passed in 1807. However, some Southerners ignored the new ruling and continued to smuggle slaves in through the ports.

FREE BLACKS

Anti-slavery laws, private manumissions, that is grants of freedom by individual slave-owners, and the emancipation by grateful state governments of black slaves who had fought the British, all led to a rise in the number of free blacks. Some slaves were also able to purchase their own freedom. But liberation did not mean equality.

The North-South Divide

Statistics tell the story, and show the North-South divide very clearly. In 1800, 26 per cent of the black population in the northern state of New York was free, but by 1830, this figure was 100 per cent. By contrast, free blacks in South Carolina made up 2 per cent of the population in 1800. This figure had *fallen* to 1 per cent in 1830 because the states of the Deep South had become fiercely pro-slavery and passed laws making manumission more difficult.

About 60 per cent of free blacks lived in towns and cities such as New York. Most found employment in low-paid jobs, for example as dockers and maids. However, a few became wealthy. Among them was Paul Cuffee, a ship-builder and landowner from the northern state of Massachusetts.

BELOW *Martin Robinson Delany (1812-1885) was the grandson of slaves. He studied law and medicine at Harvard University and became a notable doctor, author and anti-slavery activist.*

Discrimination and Resistance

Public laws and personal prejudice blighted the lives of free blacks both in the North and in the South. In the 1800s, state after state stopped them from voting – by 1840, 93 per cent of black people could not vote. They were also barred from many jobs.

Faced with such discrimination, free blacks acted. As white churches shunned them, they founded their own, for example the Bethel Church for Negro Methodists (1793). As white schools and clubs

LEFT *Many African-American churches were founded because black people were not welcomed in white-run religious establishments. But many continue to flourish because their members enjoy the style of worship and sense of community to be experienced there. This present-day choir of African Americans is singing at the Bethel Church, Virginia.*

turned them away, they built their own. And as white newspapers ignored their concerns, they wrote their own, such as *Freedom's Journal* (1827). Some free blacks did not think that their lives would ever improve in the USA. So they emigrated to Liberia, a West African republic established for them in 1821 by the American Colonization Society.

? PEOPLE IN QUESTION

Louisiana Creoles

'Creole' is the name given to American-born black slaves (see page 29). However, it can also refer to free people of mixed African and European descent, and especially to mixed-race people from Louisiana and other southern states whose white ancestors were French or Spanish. (Louisiana was at different times a French and a Spanish colony.)

Creoles sometimes thought of themselves as a 'third race'. They were free blacks, yet unlike most were usually French-speaking Roman Catholics. In addition, they were often light-skinned, with European features. Many deliberately set themselves apart from darker-skinned free blacks, and some owned slaves.

In the past, many people thought that skin colour was a major defining characteristic of Creoles. But some experts, including Creole Sybil Kein, now question this view. They argue that Creole culture – the literature, music, even cookery of this distinctive group – gives a far greater insight into who they were.

ABOLITION IN BRITAIN

BELOW *A violent scene from the French Revolution. The revolutionary government passed a law allowing slaves on the French-ruled island of St Domingue to vote, but it was ignored by the planters. As a result, the slaves rebelled in 1791. The French eventually captured their leader, Toussaint L'Ouverture, but the island was granted independence in 1804.*

As in the USA, so in Britain, anti-slavery sentiment began to increase markedly during the late eighteenth century. In 1772 Lord Mansfield, the Lord Chief Justice of England, ruled that a slave called James Somerset could not be forced to leave England by his master. This judgement led to a fierce debate about the morality of slavery. In 1787, Quakers, Baptists and others who found it repugnant set up the Abolition Society. Their first aim was to end the slave trade.

Through making speeches and publishing tracts, the Society won widespread backing. But there were also other reasons for the public's anti-slavery mood. The French Revolution (1789-99), whose leaders opposed slavery, had stirred up ideas of liberty and equality in Britain. New economic theories, in particular Scottish philosopher Adam Smith's argument that unpaid slave labour was inefficient, were also influential.

Planters and slave-traders from ports such as Liverpool hit back. They claimed the trade was vital for Britain's economy, and supplied parliament with evidence to support their case.

The Road to Abolition

At first, parliament favoured the slave-traders. It did not want to lead the country into financial ruin, or to encourage the spread of revolution from France and French-ruled St Domingue (modern day Haiti), where a slave rebellion had erupted in 1791. However two abolitionists in particular kept up the pressure. Thomas Clarkson went to the slaving ports of Liverpool and Bristol to collect damning evidence about the slave trade. MP (Member of Parliament) William Wilberforce then used this information in his parliamentary speeches. Wilberforce proposed many parliamentary resolutions for the abolition of the slave trade. One was passed in 1806, and Britain's Atlantic trade came to an end the following year.

? PEOPLE IN QUESTION

Olaudah Equiano (c.1745-1797)

Olaudah Equiano claimed to have been born in West Africa, and to have been kidnapped by slavers at the age of about ten. After supposedly serving two masters in the Americas and acquiring a new name, Gustavus Vassa, he purchased his freedom in 1766. In 1789, by now settled in London, Equiano published an account of his experiences called *The Interesting Narrative of the Life of Olaudah Equiano, or Gustavus Vassa the African, Written by Himself*. An ardent campaigner against the slave trade, Equiano travelled around Britain selling his book and making abolitionist speeches. He died in about 1797.

There has long been a debate about whether Equiano was the author of the book published under his name. White abolitionists often wrote ex-slaves' stories for them, and some experts claim the Africa-born Equiano would not have known English well enough to create the book alone. More recent research has posed another question, namely was the book's story true? Before its publication, Equiano had said he was born in South Carolina, USA, and his baptismal record supports this view. Now some experts believe he invented his African past to provide material for his abolitionist campaigns.

ABOVE *Olaudah Equiano, a campaigner against the slave trade, as he appears on the frontispiece of his book.*

The Industrial Revolution

Slavery stimulated the British economy. Money from British banks poured into the Americas to make the purchase of slaves and the establishment of plantations possible. The buying and selling of slave-produced crops then yielded great profits, which fuelled yet more investment. At the same time, people of the Americas and Africa bought large quantities of British products such as textiles. Industry responded by increasing its output, which by the 1750s was worth about £1.26 million per year.

Britain's Industrial Revolution began during the eighteenth century, when these important changes were taking place. Some historians suggest that this was in part due to slavery, which stimulated demand and provided huge profits for investment in new factories. Others question whether the link is so direct. But all agree that slavery transformed Western economies. In *Transatlantic Slavery* (1994), Stephen Small (see page 18) expresses this view as follows:

It was this [slave] *labour that fed financial accumulation* [the making and saving of large sums of money], *economic expansion and the base for industrial acquisition, that is, the development of capitalism.*

CHANGING TIMES

The end of the slave trade meant that the British Caribbean received no more African slaves. Abolitionists had hoped masters would therefore treat existing slaves better, but they were disappointed. Far from improving, many slaves' lives worsened after 1807. As no new slaves were arriving to do farmwork, hundreds who had been working as house servants were forced back into the fields.

RIGHT *A new slave punishment, the treadmill, was first used in Trinidad in 1823, and was soon introduced in the other British-ruled Caribbean islands. Slaves had to turn the mill with their feet at great speed.*

LEFT *Thomas Clarkson gives a passionate speech to the World Anti-Slavery Convention, in 1840. Although Clarkson is less famous than Wilberforce, his contribution to the abolitionist cause was equally vital.*

Slaves were also *choosing* to alter their lives. In particular, many were becoming Christians, often Baptists. Church membership gave these slaves a sense of common purpose, and many now joined together in open rebellion. At Easter 1816, for example, slaves rose up in Barbados, while in the winter of 1831-2, Jamaican slaves staged a revolt known as the Baptist War.

A NEW BRITAIN

Back in Britain, Wilberforce, Clarkson and others set up the Anti-Slavery Society in 1823 to oppose slavery itself. Meanwhile, the Industrial Revolution was causing thousands to leave the countryside to find work in city factories. This population move-ment was among the reasons for the 1832 Reform Act. It gave more men, especially city industrialists, the right to vote. As most of them believed in the free trade ideas of Adam Smith (see page 38) and considered slave-owning outdated, many pro-slavery MPs soon lost their seats.

Spurred on by a supportive public and anti-slavery prime min-ister Lord Grey, the abolitionists now redoubled their efforts to end slavery itself. The chief parliamentary activist was Thomas Buxton, whose Emancipation Bill was passed in 1833 and became effective on 31 July 1834. Planters received £20 million to ease any financial hurt they might suffer, while adult slaves still had to serve them as unpaid 'apprentices' for several more years. But on 31 July 1838, slaves' freedom became joyfully complete.

? EVENT IN QUESTION

Who – or what – caused abolition?

For many years after the Emancipation Act, most historians believed that it was committed abolitionists such as Clarkson, Wilberforce and Buxton who were primarily responsible for ending British slavery. More recently, experts have emphasized the underlying social and economic causes of abolition. In *Transatlantic Slavery* (1994), James Walvin makes a plea for balance:

The temptation of modern scholars is to see the abolition of the British slave system merely as a function of [dependent on] broadly based economic and social changes in Britain and the Caribbean ... Yet there has been a danger, in recent years, of undervaluing the abolitionist movement, and its prominent leaders. In truth they played a crucial role, for they acted as a catalyst, capitalising on these broader changes, often unconsciously. It was, after all, Parliament which abolished the slave trade and slavery.

THE FREE CARIBBEAN

Slavery was dead, but planters still had great power, since they owned large areas of land. At first, many slaves had little choice but to keep working for them. They were paid low wages and charged high rents for cabins where they had once lived for nothing. To escape this stranglehold, ex-slaves had to get their own land. Some bought it from the British government. Others moved into free villages, which were often built on land purchased by missionaries.

SUGAR SLUMP

As people left the sugar estates, planters found that they no longer had enough workers. Some reacted by introducing steam mills, which made the work less labour-intensive. Others imported indentured labourers from new sources, particularly the British colony of India.

Planters had other problems, too. The British government, now committed to free trade, wanted to abolish import duties on foreign goods. Such duties made sugar from Cuba and Brazil

more expensive than Caribbean sugar. But after the 1846 Sugar Duties Act, Caribbean sugar became equally costly, sales slumped and fortunes were lost. A Jamaica plantation worth £80,000 in the 1830s sold for £500 in 1849.

ABOVE *Slaves planting sugar cane in the Bahamas in the early nineteenth century.*

The sugar industry revived in the 1850s. But the presence of cheap Indian labour meant whites refused to increase ex-slaves' wages. Bad pay and conditions led many black people to revolt. The worst rebellion took place in Morant Bay, Jamaica, in 1865, but was crushed. Afterwards, Jamaica and other British Caribbean islands were made Crown Colonies ruled more directly by the government in London. In the 1880s, rising sales of cheap French and German sugar made from beet not cane caused another slump and the collapse of more plantations.

43

THE SPREAD OF SLAVERY IN THE US

Abolition of the slave trade in the USA was not, as in Britain, a prelude to the end of slavery. On the contrary, slavery became more widespread from the late eighteenth century. This time cotton, not sugar, was to blame.

Moving West

Until the 1790s, US planters had grown cotton mainly on plantations in South Carolina and Georgia. Their crop was long-staple cotton, which thrived in the semi-tropical conditions of those states but not elsewhere. Short-staple cotton, by contrast, was able to grow in a far wider range of climates. However, it was unprofitable as it was very time-consuming to remove this plant's sticky seeds from the fibres used to make cloth.

This situation changed in 1793 when a man called Eli Whitney invented the cotton gin ('gin' is an abbreviation of 'engine'), a machine that removed cotton seeds fifty times faster than possible by hand. Demand for cotton was high, especially from Britain where the Industrial Revolution had led to the building of many textile factories. Short-staple cotton cultivation therefore soon spread west into Alabama, Mississippi, Arkansas,

? EVENT IN QUESTION

Underground Railroad escapes

By 1804, when cotton was spreading across the South, all the northern states had abolished slavery (see pages 34-35). Slaves had always run away, but with the free North beckoning, the practice became more common. The US government therefore introduced a Fugitive Slave Law in 1850. It let Southerners bring escapees back from the North.

Gradually, a system was established to help slaves make their way from South to North. Called the Underground Railroad, it was a network of 'safe houses' where slaves could stay, and to which they were led by free blacks known as conductors.

It is hard for experts to be sure how many slave escapes conductors made possible. Investigations suggest that few slaves successfully fled the Deep South. About 1,000 slaves per year left the Upper South in the pre-Civil War era, but not all used the Underground Railroad.

Louisiana and Texas. The rise in output was huge. In 1792, the South had produced just 13,000 bales. By 1860, it was churning out 4.8 million bales per year.

The Interstate Slave Trade

The new cotton plantations were worked by slaves using the gang system (see pages 26-27). Between 1793 and 1807, about 250,000 were brought from Africa. But once the transatlantic slave trade ended, this source dried up, and trade between states developed instead. Virginia and Maryland were specially active in this commerce, as failing tobacco crops (see page 24) meant they were short of money but had slaves to spare. They therefore sold thousands to planters further south, often callously separating husbands from wives and parents from children.

ABOVE *Harriet Tubman (far left) was the most celebrated Underground Railroad conductor. Born a slave, she escaped from her master in Maryland in 1849, and in the years before abolition led about 300 slaves to the North.*

CHAPTER 4

The American Civil War

In the nineteenth century, the USA spread steadily west. The debate about whether slavery should extend into its new lands ultimately led to war.

THE MISSOURI COMPROMISE

BELOW *The 1820 Missouri Compromise established where slavery would be allowed in the ever expanding USA.*

By 1819, the USA had 11 slave states and 11 free states. When the new territory of Missouri applied to become a state, it was clear that this balance would be lost. Southerners wanted Missouri to be a slave state, Northerners wanted it to be free, so in 1820 the US Congress reached a compromise. Missouri would join the Union (USA) as a slave state, Maine, newly separated

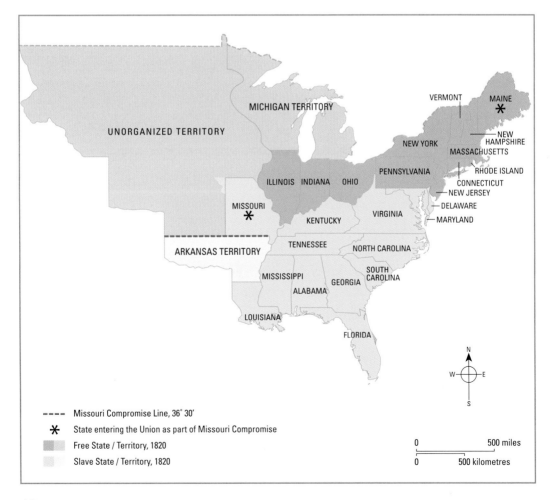

- - - - Missouri Compromise Line, 36° 30′
✳ State entering the Union as part of Missouri Compromise
Free State / Territory, 1820
Slave State / Territory, 1820

0   500 miles
0   500 kilometres

from Massachusetts, as a free state. Senators also banned the intro-
duction of slavery above a line extending west from Missouri's
southern border (see map). Meanwhile, abolition pressure grew
and in 1833 the American Anti-Slavery Society was founded.

DEEPENING DIVISIONS

In the 1840s, the USA won territory in the south-west from
Mexico. Again, there were arguments about whether the land
should be divided into slave or free states, but in 1850 a new
compromise was reached. It stated California (see map page 49)
should be free, but that there should be no ban on slavery in the
rest of the new land.

In 1854, the same problem erupted further east. According
to the Missouri Compromise, slavery should have been illegal
in the Kansas and Nebraska territories. But hoping to avoid
conflict, Senator for Illinois, Stephen Douglas, proposed a bill
that would allow the people who settled the lands to vote on the
slavery issue. Southern politicians agreed to support Douglas
only if he proposed the abolition of the Missouri Compromise,
too. His bill passed into law as the 1854 Kansas-Nebraska Act.

Outraged, some Northern politicians formed a new anti-
slavery party, the Republican Party. In 1860 its presidential candidate, Abraham Lincoln, was elected.

? EVENT IN QUESTION

The Nat Turner rebellion

The first half of the nineteenth century was a time of slave rebellions in the South. The most serious
revolt of the era occurred in Virginia in 1831. It was led by Nat Turner, a slave who believed he was
inspired by God. He and his mob were stopped only after they had murdered about 59 whites. Turner
and 10 of his associates were hanged, and about 120 others killed in reprisal.

The Nat Turner rebellion prompted a backlash in the South and many new laws designed to curb
slaves' rights were introduced. Largely as a result, there were no more major revolts before the Civil
War. The question some historians ask about this episode is whether slaves were too terrified to
rebel any more, or simply too clever. The consensus now is that slaves realized they were unlikely to
be able to overthrow whites on their own, so returned to less confrontational forms of resistance,
such as working slowly or pretending to be ill.

THE UNION AND THE CONFEDERACY

By late 1860, all attempts at compromise between North and South had failed. Now the conflict turned into open warfare. Between December 1860 and February 1861, seven southern states declared that they had seceded from the USA and so were

? PEOPLE IN QUESTION

Abraham Lincoln (1809–1865)

Abraham Lincoln has always been the subject of debate. In modern times there is great argument about whether he was a racist. The question is hard to resolve, as some of his speeches suggest that he was, others that he was not. In July 1858, for example, he said:

Let us discard all this quibbling about ... this race and that race ... being inferior ... Let us ... unite as one people throughout this land, until we shall once more stand up declaring that all men are created equal.

But just two months later, this was the view that Lincoln expressed:

I will say, then, that I am not ... in favor of bringing about ... the social and political equality of the white and black races ... there must be the position of superior and inferior, and I ... am in favor of having the superior position assigned to the white race.

LEFT *Abraham Lincoln is remembered particularly for his role in the Civil War, for the Emancipation Proclamation, and for the Gettysburg Address, a speech he made on 19 November 1863 in which he committed himself to 'government of the people, by the people, for the people.'*

no longer part of the Union. Then they joined together in a new body called the Confederacy, led by Jefferson Davis. War broke out between the Confederacy and the Union in April, leading four more slave states to join the Confederate side. Its capital was established in Richmond, Virginia.

President Abraham Lincoln did not lead the Union states into the war to end slavery. As the Republican candidate in 1860, he had promised only to stop the *expansion* of slavery into new lands. His one war aim in 1861 was to force Confederate states back into the Union.

A Difference of Opinion

Soon after the war started, some of Lincoln's military commanders began to free slaves in Confederate areas that their armies had occupied. To these commanders, the slaves were just 'contraband of war', like land and goods. The President, however, disagreed and twice ordered his soldiers to return captured slaves. The reason was simple. Lincoln believed that slavery was morally wrong, but he did not want to lose the support of the four (later five) slave-holding states loyal to the Union by setting slaves free. Emancipation was still not part of his plans.

BELOW *During the Civil War, 11 slave states left the Union to form the Confederacy. But five slave states remained loyal and fought their fellow slave owners.*

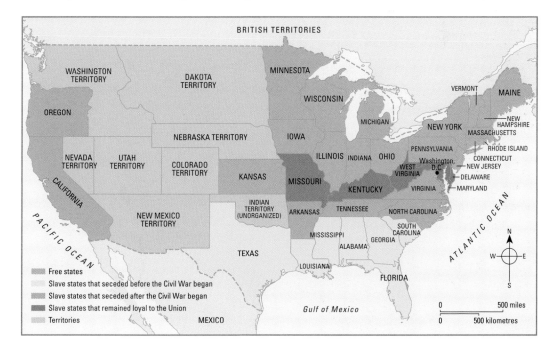

THE WAR DRAGS ON

As 1862 progressed, both sides' hope of a rapid victory faded. It was now clear that the struggle would be long, bitter and bloody. Faced with this grim prospect, free white men became far less eager to join the Union forces. By contrast, thousands of Southern slaves who had fled to the Union armies for refuge were keen to become soldiers. However, they were banned from enlisting because of their slave status.

Lincoln now began to realize that the emancipation of slaves would not only provide him with more, much-needed soldiers, but also bring other benefits. In particular, it would turn the war into a struggle for abolition, a noble cause for which whites might again be willing to fight. It would also severely damage the slave-dependent southern economy, and so reduce Confederate strength.

BELOW *A group of contraband slaves, on land captured by the Union Army await news of their future.*

THE EMANCIPATION PROCLAMATION

Lincoln slowly edged towards making abolition a second war aim. Then, on 22 September 1862, he issued the preliminary Emancipation Proclamation. It stated that unless the Confederacy ended its struggle within 100 days, he would outlaw slavery. There was no reply, so on 1 January 1863, Lincoln made the final Emancipation Proclamation. It declared that slaves in rebel areas 'are, and henceforward shall be, free'.

About 100,000 ex-slaves from the South now rushed to fight for the Union. Like the similar number of Northern blacks, they served in segregated units and were paid less than whites. But regiments such as the 54th Massachusetts Colored distinguished themselves in battle.

TWO ENDINGS

The Emancipation Proclamation did not abolish slavery everywhere – it remained legal in slave states loyal to the Union. But in December 1865, eight months after the war ended in victory for the Union, the 13th Amendment to the Constitution brought nationwide abolition.

? WHAT IF...

There had been no war?

Experts often discuss what would have happened if the Union had accepted the secession of the Confederacy and no war had followed. In his book *Without Consent or Contract* (1989), American historian Robert W. Fogel (see page 24) states that in his view, the failure of abolition in the South would have damaged not only other anti-slavery campaigns but also other reform movements, such as British efforts to extend voting rights to more people.

Fogel claims, too, that the Confederacy would have grown wealthy, thanks largely to its cotton industry, and would have become a world power with a strong army. The annexation of nearby countries such as Cuba might then have followed. The rise of the South would also have damaged the economy of the North.

Not all historians agree with Fogel's analysis. Many claim civil war was inevitable, and that if it had occurred later, a better-prepared Confederacy would have won.

CHAPTER 5

Reconstruction and After

The divided, battle-scarred Union now had to be put back together. Both the process and the period of rebuilding are known as Reconstruction.

DEATH AND DIVISION

Abraham Lincoln was assassinated on 9 April 1865 and replaced by former Vice-President Andrew Johnson. A Southerner, Johnson had not opposed slavery, but had accepted its abolition. He was determined, however, to stop blacks winning equal rights, saying 'white men alone must govern the South'.

Johnson introduced Reconstruction in May 1865. Each former Confederate state now had to draw up a constitution that accepted the 13th Amendment. They did so, but none of the new constitutions gave blacks the right to vote. The situation worsened in the autumn when some states introduced 'Black Codes' that discriminated against blacks, for example by prescribing harsher punishments for them than whites.

RADICAL RECONSTRUCTION

Congress struck back by introducing its own plan, known as Radical Reconstruction. Two new amendments to the Constitution were passed, the 14th (ratified 1868) making black people full citizens of the USA, and the 15th (ratified 1870), allowing them to vote. Meanwhile in 1867, the South was divided into five military districts and the army sent in to take control. Now states had to introduce constitutions that accepted the 13th, 14th and 15th Amendments before they could return to the Union.

Once the states had done so, black people were able to play a part in Southern governments for the first time. They were most strongly represented in South Carolina, where there were

87 blacks in the first Reconstruction-era government. At national level, 16 black people were elected to Congress between 1869 and 1880.

THE END OF AN ERA

Southerners bitterly opposed to the new governments now began to use violence to stop black people participating in elections, while at the same time encouraging more whites to vote. As a result, blacks were driven out of state legislatures and laws were passed to restrict their rights again.

A grubby compromise finally brought Reconstruction to an end. In 1877, the Republican presidential candidate Rutherford B. Hayes needed the support of Southerners to win. They agreed to give it only if troops left the South. The soldiers were gone that year.

ABOVE *One of the black men who was a member of the US Congress during Reconstruction. Experts are not sure who it is, but it may be Robert Smalls, a former South Carolina slave who famously seized a Confederate ship during the Civil War and handed it over to the Union.*

? EVENT IN QUESTION

Change in the South

Like a massive earthquake, the Civil War and the destruction of slavery permanently altered the landscape of Southern life.

These are the words of distinguished American historian Eric Foner. Many other experts agree with him, pointing out the major changes that occurred in the South during and after Reconstruction. Among them were increasing industrialization, a new acceptance of capitalism by planters, and the opening up of educational opportunities for black people – a government organization called the Freedmen's Bureau (1865-72) established over 4,000 new schools. Other experts, however, claim that much really stayed the same. In particular, the South remained poorer and less industrial than the North, while black people still suffered fierce discrimination and prejudice. Many also had little choice but to continue working for wealthy white landowners.

ABOVE *During the Jim Crow era, black people like this man in Oklahoma were not allowed to use even the same drinking fountains as white people.*

JIM CROW LAWS

In the late 1870s, Southerners began to use the courts to deny black Americans their rights. The so-called Jim Crow laws that they passed were named after a black character featured in racist musical shows. Despite the 15th Amendment, many Jim Crow laws set out to stop black people voting. Some states, for example, introduced literacy clauses, which said that blacks could vote only if their reading and writing was of a certain standard. As many had been denied education, they could not reach the necessary level. Other states passed laws requiring people to pay a poll tax before they could vote. Many blacks did not have enough money, and therefore could not vote.

Other Jim Crow laws segregated blacks from whites by making them use separate schools and other public facilities, or different areas of the same facilities, for example, different carriages in trains. Between 1875 and 1900, segregation laws were passed in every Southern state.

Booker T.(Taliaferro) Washington (1856-1915) and W.E.B. (William Edward Burghardt) Du Bois (1868-1963)

Washington and Du Bois both campaigned for black rights during the Jim Crow era. But they disagreed about the best way to win them, and so stirred up much public debate.

Washington was born a slave, but after abolition became a teacher. In 1881 he was made head of the Tuskegee Institute, Alabama, which offered tuition in 30 trades. Washington thought the best way forward for black people was to prove themselves first as manual workers, rather than to push for social justice. As he declared in 1895:

The wisest among my race understand that the agitation of questions of social equality is the extremest folly ... It is at the bottom of life that we must begin, and not at the top.

Du Bois was born in Massachusetts. After attending Harvard University, where he obtained a doctorate in history, he became a prominent member of the NAACP, as well as a distinguished academic sociologist. In books such as *The Souls of Black Folk* (1903), he denounced Washington's ideas, claiming that blacks had every right to demand social equality and seek professional careers. He believed in the motto of the Niagara Movement, the forerunner of the NAACP. This was:

Persistent manly agitation is the way to liberty.

THE FIGHTBACK

Black people's efforts to win back their rights met with little success. The case of Louisiana carpenter Homer A. Plessy seemed to seal black people's fate. When he appealed against his arrest for sitting in a whites-only train carriage, the US Supreme Court ruled against him. Its 1896 ruling said segregation was acceptable as long as facilities for blacks were 'separate but equal'. They rarely were, but the authorities ignored complaints.

Among the groups set up to fight this discrimination was the National Association for the Advancement of Colored People (NAACP), in 1910. In 1954, together with the parents of a black girl called Linda Brown, the NAACP won a landmark case. The parents claimed that the Board of Education in Topeka, Kansas, could not make their daughter attend a segregated school, as segregation infringed their rights as US citizens, violating the 14th Amendment. The US Supreme Court agreed, and the foundations of the Jim Crow laws began to shake.

THE CIVIL RIGHTS MOVEMENT

After the Brown ruling the black civil rights campaign began to make real progress.

BELOW *Martin Luther King was a gifted orator. In a celebrated speech of 1963, he spoke about his dream of a future where racial harmony would reign across the USA.*

On 1 December 1955 in Montgomery, Alabama, NAACP member Rosa Parks refused to give up her bus seat to a white man. As this was against local segregation laws, she was arrested. Black activists, such as Baptist minister Martin Luther King, organized a bus boycott in protest. It continued until 21 December 1956, when the US Supreme Court declared the state's seating laws unconstitutional.

? PEOPLE IN QUESTION

Martin Luther King (1929–1968)

Martin Luther King was born in Atlanta, Georgia, and as a young man became a Baptist preacher. His involvement in the civil rights movement began during the Montgomery bus boycott, when he was minister of the city's Dexter Avenue Baptist Church, and he eventually became one of its leading figures. King's achievements were recognized in 1964, when he won the Nobel Prize for Peace.

Experts accept that King played a major role in the civil rights movement. However, many now question whether that role has been exaggerated, and the contributions of other leaders and local activists have therefore been downplayed. This view was expressed by Ella Baker, former associate director of the SCLC (see below), when she said:

The movement made Martin rather than Martin making the movement.

THE SCLC AND SNCC

In 1957, King set up an organization to campaign for laws that would give black people equal rights. He called it the Southern Christian Leadership Conference (SCLC), and intended it to use only non-violent methods. In 1960, student activists established another campaigning group. This was the Student Non-Violent Co-ordinating Committee (SNCC).

The two groups ran many events. A 1963 protest march in Birmingham, Alabama, prompted US President John F. Kennedy to submit a civil rights bill to Congress. As he was assassinated the same year, President Lyndon B. Johnson signed the Civil Rights Act into law in 1964. It banned public segregation, but did not fully guarantee black people the right to vote.

King and other activists therefore next launched a voting rights campaign. In August 1965, a Voting Rights Act was passed that outlawed literacy tests in most states and promised the federal (national) government would send officials to help black people register to vote.

BLACK POWER!

Despite the new laws, discrimination remained widespread, so campaigning continued. However many SNCC members, influenced by radicals such as Black Muslim Malcolm X, were losing faith in non-violence. Finally, during a 1966 march, SNCC leader Stokely Carmichael used the slogan 'Black Power!', and seemed to encourage physical conflict. In 1968 the SNCC and the SCLC split, and after King's assassination the same year, black activism lost much of its focus.

LEFT *Following the Brown ruling many US schools opened their doors to black children for the first time. This was the scene in Thompson Elementary School, Washington D.C.*

Consequences of Slavery

The consequences of the African-American slave trade, and the institution of slavery that it served, cast a long shadow across four continents – Africa, North and South America, and Europe. Although nearly a century-and-a-half has passed since both were outlawed in Britain and North America (Brazil did not ban slavery until 1888), a deep-rooted legacy remains.

Mind and Memory

Among the most important aspects of this legacy is the impact it has had on people's minds. This of course, depends on whether the person concerned is black or white. Stephen Small (see page 18) argues that many black people can never forget what their slave ancestors suffered, and so carry their history with them. Many whites, by contrast, know little about slavery, and do not care to think about the suffering that some of their ancestors caused.

Inequality and Racism

In the USA black people, now usually known as African Americans, make up about 12 per cent of the population. Despite the civil rights gains of the 1960s and more recent campaigns such as affirmative action programmes to make jobs and college places more accessible, statistics prove that they still suffer inequality and disadvantage. In 1994, for example, the black unemployment level was 13.9 per cent, white just 6.7 per cent. The current average income of African American families is $18,098 per year, of white families $30,853.

Most experts agree that racism is one of the main reasons for this inequality. Despite the fact that African Americans are both willing and able to play a full role in society – indeed one, Colin Powell, became US Secretary of State in 2000 – they still suffer discrimination. The same is true in Britain, where many descendants of Caribbean slaves have lived since the 1950s. After the murder of black teenager Stephen Lawrence in 1993, London's Metropolitan Police was found to be 'institutionally racist', and other groups, such as the army, have been similarly criticized.

AFRICA AND REPARATIONS

The impact of the slave trade on Africa was enormous (see page 18), and organizations such as the African World Reparations and Repatriation Truth Commission are demanding financial compensation (reparations) for the continent. In the USA, a team of lawyers may take the federal government to court to demand over $4 trillion for the descendants of slaves living in the country.

The backlash has been furious, with American academics and journalists highlighting what they see as the flaws in the reparations plan. They point out, for example, that most present-day white Americans are descended from immigrants who arrived after the abolition of slavery, so bear no real responsibility for it.

But calmer voices suggest the slave trade was so complex that it cannot be reduced to a simple story of whites against blacks. Instead it would be wiser to work together against racism and poverty, and so erase the trade's sorry legacy.

ABOVE *A positive image of African Americans in society in 2002. Colin Powell, the US Secretary of State, talks with Condoleezza Rice, the US National Security Advisor.*

59

Timeline

1619
First black Africans, a group of 20, brought to North America.

1665
English occupy Cape Coast fort on West African coast.

1756-1763
Seven Years' War. British victory means French lose colonies in North America.

1775
American Revolution begins.

1776
JULY: Declaration of Independence issued in North America.

1777
Vermont becomes first US state to ban slavery.

1780s
Slave trade's busiest decade; about 80,000 people taken from Africa each year.

1783
American Revolution ends in British defeat and withdrawal.

1785
Manumission Society founded in New York.

1787
Abolition Society founded in Britain.

1789-1799
French Revolution takes place.

1791
Slave rebellion in St Domingue (modern Haiti).

1793
Eli Whitney invents cotton gin.

1799
State of New York bans slavery.

1804
New Jersey becomes the last state in American North to ban slavery.

1806
Britain passes law banning the slave trade from 1807.

1807
USA passes law banning the slave trade from 1808.

1816
Slave rebellion in Barbados.

1820
Missouri Compromise introduced in USA.

1821
West African republic of Liberia founded as home for free slaves.

1823
Anti-Slavery Society founded in Britain.

1831
Nat Turner slave rebellion in Virginia, USA.

1831-1832
'Baptist War' slave revolt in Jamaica.

1833
Britain passes Emancipation Bill. American Anti-Slavery Society founded.

1834
Apprenticeship replaces slavery in British colonies.

1838
JULY: Apprenticeship abolished and slavery ends in British colonies .

1846
Britain passes Sugar Duties Act, removing import taxes on foreign sugar.

1850
USA passes Fugitive
Slave Law.

1854
USA passes Kansas-
Nebraska Act.

1860
Abraham Lincoln becomes
first Republican president of
USA.

1861-1865
American Civil War, Northern
(Union) states triumph over
Southern (Confederate) states.

1862
SEPTEMBER: Preliminary
Emancipation Proclamation.

1863
JANUARY: Final Emancipation
Proclamation.

1865
Abraham Lincoln
assassinated.
Reconstruction begins.
13th Amendment to US
Constitution outlaws
slavery nationwide.
Morant Bay rebellion
in Jamaica.

1865-1872
Freedmen's Bureau
in operation.

1868
14th Amendment to
constitution makes black
people full US citizens.

1870
15th Amendment to
constitution allows black
people to vote.

1875-1900
Segregation laws introduced in
every state of the American
South.

1877
Reconstruction (started 1867)
ended. Troops leave South.

1888
Slavery banned in Brazil.

1896
US Supreme Court judgement
in Homer A. Plessy case rules
segregation acceptable if black
facilities 'separate but equal'.

1910
National Association for the
Advancement of Colored
People (NAACP) founded.

1954
NAACP wins landmark
Brown v. *Board of Education of
Topeka* case.

1955-1956
Montgomery bus boycott
in Alabama.

1957
Southern Christian
Leadership Conference
(SCLC) founded.

1960
Student Non-Violent
Co-ordinating Committee
(SNCC) founded.

1963
Civil rights march in
Birmingham, Alabama.

1964
USA passes Civil Rights Act.

1965
Selma to Montgomery civil
rights march.
USA Passes Voting
Rights Act.

1966
'Black Power!' slogan coined by
SNCC leader Stokely
carmichael.

1968
APRIL: Martin Luther King
assassinated.

61

Glossary

abolitionist A person who campaigns for the abolition of the slave trade and/or slavery.

Anglican Of or belonging to the Church of England or an associated church.

Berber A member of an ancient North African people that adopted Islam during the seventh century CE.

bight A wide curving bay.

Black Muslim A member of the Nation of Islam, a black religious group sharing some beliefs with orthodox Islam and founded in the USA in 1930.

boycott A form of protest that usually involves refusing to carry out a particular activity or to purchase particular goods.

colonialism The policy of taking over and ruling other countries, which are then known as colonies.

Congress The law-making body of the USA. It consists of a lower house, the House of Representatives, and an upper house, the Senate.

cotton gin A machine designed to remove the seeds from cotton pods (bolls) so that the remaining fibres can be spun. 'Gin' is short for 'engine'.

Creole A black person born in the Americas or a person from Louisiana of mixed black and white European (French or Spanish) parentage.

Crown Colony A British colony ruled directly from London and subject to laws made there.

Deep South The south-eastern US states of South Carolina, Georgia, Alabama, Mississippi and sometimes also Louisiana.

emancipation Freedom or the process of setting free.

English Civil War A war between people who wanted England to remain a monarchy under Charles I and people who wanted the country to become a republic. The conflict lasted from 1642 to 1651.

feudal Of a hierarchical society in which each group owes service to the one above.

French Revolution The 10-year period (1789 to 1799) during which the French monarchy was overthrown and replaced by a republic.

hierarchical (of a society) Arranged in fixed ranks or classes, with rulers at the top and usually poor peasants at the bottom.

Hispaniola A large Caribbean island that Christopher Columbus named, and claimed for Spain, in 1492.

import duty Tax on goods brought into a country.

legislature The law-making body of a government.

Louisiana A French colony in North America that was founded in 1699 and comprised a huge area around the Mississippi River.

manumission A grant of freedom to a slave, either given freely by an owner or purchased by a slave.

New England The most north-easterly part of the USA, now comprising the states of Maine, New Hampshire, Vermont, Massachusetts, Rhode Island and Connecticut.

planter A plantation owner.

reparations Compensation for past wrongs in the form of money, goods or actions.

savannah Dry grassland, usually with a few bushes and trees scattered across its surface.

secede from To leave formally.

Senate The upper of the two houses that make up the US Congress.

Seven Years' War A war fought from 1756 to 1763 between Britain and Prussia on one side and Austria, France, Sweden and Russia on the other.

tract A pamphlet, usually expressing strong views about a political, moral or religious issue.

Union The USA considered as a collection of states joined together under one national government. During the American Civil War, only the Northern states were known as the Union, as the Southern states had seceded.

US Supreme Court The highest federal (national) court in the USA. It is made up of nine judges and its rulings take precedence over any made in state courts.

Further information

BOOKS

Curtin/Feierman/Thompson/Vansina, *African History* (Longman Group Limited, 1995) This general survey of African history contains a detailed chapter (Chapter 7) by Philip Curtin on West Africa during the slave trade era. Several other chapters also contain relevant information.

Jonathan Earle, *The Routledge Atlas of African American History* (Routledge, 2000) Concise text illuminates the clear and very useful maps in this atlas. Slavery is well covered, and so, too, is the civil rights era and the cultural background to political events.

Paul Edwards ed., *Equiano's Travels* (Heinemann, 1970) An abridged and annotated version of Olaudah Equiano's book (see page 39). Despite doubts about the authenticity of some of the narrative, there is much to learn about slavery from this edition.

Robert W. Fogel and Stanley L. Engerman, *Time on the Cross: The Economics of American Negro Slavery* (W.W. Norton and Company) Robert W. Fogel, *Without Consent or Contract* (W.W. Norton and Company)

Peter Kolchin, *American Slavery* (Hill & Wang, 2003) An excellent, concise survey of slavery in North America from the arrival of the first black people on the continent in 1619 to the end of Reconstruction in 1877.

Andrew Porter ed., *The Nineteenth Century* (Oxford University Press, 2001) This general survey of the British Empire during the 1800s contains a detailed chapter (Chapter 21) on the British West Indies by Gad Heuman.

Anthony Tibbles ed., *Transatlantic Slavery/Against Human Dignity* (Liverpool University Press, 2005) This catalogue was written to accompany the permanent Transatlantic Slave Trade Gallery at the Merseyside Maritime Museum in Liverpool. It contains essays on a variety of specialist topics, as well as many photographs of objects in the gallery.

Howard Zinn, *A People's History of he United States*, (Longman, 2003)

NOTE ON SOURCES

A source is information about the past. Sources can take many forms, from books, films and documents to physical objects and sound recordings.

Essentially there are two types of source, primary and secondary. Primary sources date from around the time you are studying; secondary sources, such as books like this, have been produced since that time. In general, primary sources are more immediate but contain much narrower information than secondary sources. Moreover, primary sources need handling with care.

Here are some guidelines to bear in mind when approaching a written or drawn primary source:

1. Who produced it (a politician, cartoonist, etc.?) and why? What was their motive? Were they trying to make a point?
2. When exactly was the source produced? What was going on at the time? Detail is key here, not just the year but sometimes even down to the exact time of day.
3. Might the source have been altered by an editor, censor, translator? (Possible change in translation is very important.)
4. Where was the source produced? Which country, town, region, etc?
5. Does the source tie in with other sources you have met, primary and secondary, or does it offer a new point of view?
6. Where has the source come from? Has it been selected by someone else (probably to prove a point – beware!) or did you find it through your own researches?

Index